— ULTIMATE SPORTS STATS —

GYMNASTICS
BY THE NUMBERS

Liz Sonneborn

Lerner Publications ◆ Minneapolis

Statistics are accurate through 2023.

To Kathy

Copyright © 2025 by Lerner Publishing Group, Inc.

All rights reserved. International copyright secured. No part of this book may be reproduced, stored in a retrieval system, or transmitted in any form or by any means—electronic, mechanical, photocopying, recording, or otherwise—without the prior written permission of Lerner Publishing Group, Inc., except for the inclusion of brief quotations in an acknowledged review.

Lerner Publications Company
An imprint of Lerner Publishing Group, Inc.
241 First Avenue North
Minneapolis, MN 55401 USA

For reading levels and more information, look up this title at www.lernerbooks.com.

Main body text set in Adrianna.
Typeface provided by Chank.

Editor: Annie Zheng **Designer:** Viet Chu **Photo Editor:** Cynthia Zemlicka

Library of Congress Cataloging-in-Publication Data

Names: Sonneborn, Liz, author.
Title: Gymnastics by the numbers / Liz Sonneborn.
Description: Minneapolis, MN : Lerner Publications, [2025] | Series: Ultimate sports stats (Lerner sports) | Includes bibliographical references and index. | Audience: Ages 7–11 | Audience: Grades 2–3 | Summary: "Gymnastics is taking over the world stage, but how can fans keep up with it? One way is by looking at the stats. From vault to all-around, discover how scoring works in the gymnastics world"— Provided by publisher.
Identifiers: LCCN 2023040621 (print) | LCCN 2023040622 (ebook) | ISBN 9798765625958 (library binding) | ISBN 9798765629840 (paperback) | ISBN 9798765638040 (epub)
Subjects: LCSH: Gymnastics—Juvenile literature. | Gymnastics—Records—Juvenile literature.
Classification: LCC GV461.3 .S66 2025 (print) | LCC GV461.3 (ebook) | DDC 796.44—dc23/eng/20230830

LC record available at https://lccn.loc.gov/2023040621
LC ebook record available at https://lccn.loc.gov/2023040622

Manufactured in the United States of America
1-1010068-51929-2/21/2024

TABLE OF CONTENTS

INTRODUCTION
JUDGING GYMNASTICS 4

CHAPTER 1
EVENT STATS 6

CHAPTER 2
TEAM STATS 18

CHAPTER 3
STATS ARE HERE TO STAY 24

Stats Matchup 28

Glossary 30

Learn More 31

Index 32

INTRODUCTION
JUDGING GYMNASTICS

A basketball player makes a free throw. One point. A quarterback scores a touchdown. Six points. A batter hits a home run with the bases loaded. Four runs. In artistic gymnastics, scoring is not so simple. Judges decide the scores gymnasts receive.

FREDERICK RICHARD

DIFFICULTY AND EXECUTION

Before 2006, judges gave gymnasts a single score. The highest possible was 10.00. Since 2006, judges have given gymnasts two scores. They then add them for the athlete's final score.

The D score grades the difficulty of a routine. Each move in a routine is assigned a point value based on how hard it is. The D score is the total number of points of the moves in a gymnast's routine. There is no cap on how high a D score can be.

The E score measures a routine's execution—how well the gymnast performs each move. It starts at 10.00. Judges then subtract points for mistakes.

CHENCHEN GUAN

2020 OLYMPICS WOMEN'S INDIVIDUAL EVENTS WINNERS			
EVENT	GYMNAST	D SCORE	E SCORE
Vault	Rebeca Andrade	6.000	9.266
Uneven bars	Nina Derwael	6.700	8.500
Balance beam	Chenchen Guan	6.600	8.033
Floor exercise	Jade Carey	6.300	8.066

CHAPTER 1
EVENT STATS

GIARNNI REGINI-MORAN

MEN'S FLOOR EXERCISE

Floor exercise routines are performed on a spring-loaded mat. It measures about 40 × 40 feet (12 × 12 m). The gymnast must use the entire mat area. High-scoring routines show off the gymnast's balance and strength. In 2022, British gymnast Giarnni Regini-Moran won the World Artistic Gymnastics Championships in men's floor exercise with a score of 14.533.

2022 WORLD ARTISTIC CHAMPIONSHIPS MEN'S FLOOR EXERCISE RESULTS

TEAM	GYMNAST	SCORE
Great Britain	Giarnni Regini-Moran	14.533
Japan	Daiki Hashimoto	14.500
Japan	Ryosuke Doi	14.266
France	Benjamin Osberger	14.233
Italy	Nicola Bartolini	14.233

Wait, What!?

At the 1896 Olympic Games, 10-year-old Greek gymnast Dimitrios Loundras won a bronze medal. He's the youngest Olympian in history to have won a medal.

Women's Floor Exercise

Female gymnasts also perform floor exercises. But the rules are a little different for women. Women's routines last 90 seconds. Men's routines are only 70 seconds. Women also perform to music. Men do not.

Female gymnasts highlight acrobatics and tumbling, such as somersaults, in floor routines. Women also perform dance moves in between flips and twists. Tumbling is tiring, so dance moves give gymnasts a physical and mental break.

REBECA ANDRADE

2023 World Artistic Championships Women's Floor Exercise Results

TEAM	GYMNAST	SCORE
United States	Simone Biles	14.633
Brazil	Rebeca Andrade	14.500
Brazil	Flavia Saraiva	13.966
Romania	Sabrina Maneca-Voinea	13.766
United States	Shilese Jones	13.666

WOMEN'S UNEVEN BARS

The uneven bars are a set of two bars. One is 8.2 feet (2.5 m) high. The other is 5.6 feet (1.7 m) high. Gymnasts swing from one bar to the other. The hardest moves are when a gymnast releases from a bar and then regrips it. Even a slight mistake on a release can cause a gymnast to fall. US gymnast Sunisa Lee is known for having some of the most difficult uneven bars routines.

2020 OLYMPICS WOMEN'S UNEVEN BARS RESULTS

TEAM	GYMNAST	SCORE
Belgium	Nina Derwael	15.200
Russian Olympic Committee	Anastasiia Iliankova	14.833
United States	Sunisa Lee	14.500
China	Yufei Lu	14.400
Germany	Elisabeth Seitz	14.400

SUNISA LEE

Men's Horizontal Bar

The horizontal bar requires similar skills to that of the uneven bars. The gymnast swings on a bar 9.2 feet (2.8 m) above the ground. Difficult moves involve releasing and regripping the bar. Japan's Kohei Uchimura, nicknamed King Kohei, is one of the all-time greats at the horizontal bar.

KOHEI UCHIMURA

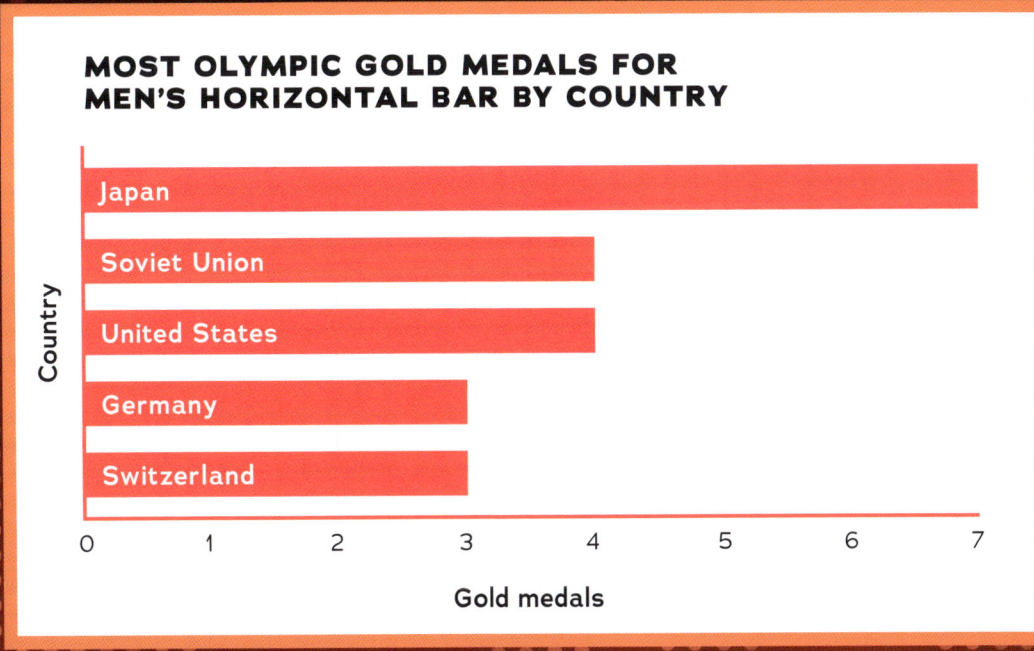

MOST OLYMPIC GOLD MEDALS FOR MEN'S HORIZONTAL BAR BY COUNTRY

MEN'S PARALLEL BARS

In the parallel bars, a gymnast grips two bars elevated 6.6 feet (2 m) above the mat. He then swings his legs above and below the bars. The event requires upper arm strength. Gymnasts have to have strength to hold one- and two-handed handstands. In 2016, Oleg Verniaiev of Ukraine snagged gold for men's parallel bars at the Olympics.

OLEG VERNIAIEV

2016 OLYMPICS MEN'S PARALLEL BARS RESULTS

TEAM	GYMNAST	SCORE
Ukraine	Oleg Verniaiev	16.041
United States	Danell Leyva	15.900
Russia	David Belyavskiy	15.783
China	Shudi Deng	15.766
Cuba	Manrique Larduet	15.625

THE PERFECT 10

Before the scoring system changed in 2006, there was one score every gymnast wanted—the perfect 10. No one had earned a 10.00 at the Olympics before 1976. That year, 14-year-old Romanian gymnast Nadia Comaneci changed the gymnastics world by getting seven perfect scores.

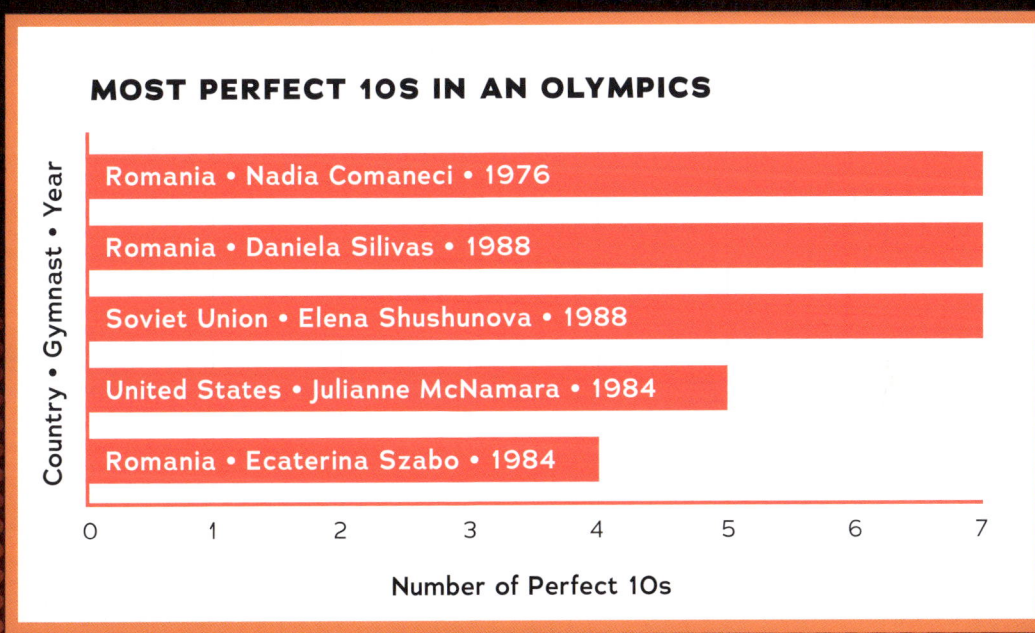

MOST PERFECT 10S IN AN OLYMPICS

Country • Gymnast • Year

- Romania • Nadia Comaneci • 1976 — 7
- Romania • Daniela Silivas • 1988 — 7
- Soviet Union • Elena Shushunova • 1988 — 7
- United States • Julianne McNamara • 1984 — 5
- Romania • Ecaterina Szabo • 1984 — 4

Number of Perfect 10s

WAIT, WHAT!?

Comaneci's perfect 10 appeared on the scoreboard as 1.00. The scoreboard was built to show only three numbers. No one had thought a gymnast could score a 10.00.

MEN'S VAULT

In men's vault, the gymnast first sprints down a runway. He then jumps on a springboard. His hands hit a vault table, hurling him into the air. After performing twists and somersaults, he must land perfectly to get a good score.

Filipino gymnast Carlos Edriel Yulo is an up-and-coming men's vault champ. He placed first in 2021 and second in 2022 at the World Championships.

CARLOS EDRIEL YULO

2021 WORLD ARTISTIC CHAMPIONSHIPS MEN'S VAULT RESULTS

TEAM	GYMNAST	SCORE
Philippines	Carlos Edriel Yulo	14.916
Japan	Hidenobu Yonekura	14.866
Israel	Andrey Medvedev	14.649
Italy	Thomas Grasso	14.549
Republic of Korea (South Korea)	Hakseon Yang	14.399

WOMEN'S VAULT

The vault is the only gymnastics event that has the same rules for men and women. Gymnasts do two vault routines for the individual competition. The final score is the average of their two scores. Romania's Monica Rosu won gold at the 2004 Olympics for women's vault by a large margin of .175 points.

MONICA ROSU

2004 OLYMPICS WOMEN'S VAULT RESULTS

TEAM	GYMNAST	SCORE
Romania	Monica Rosu	9.656
United States	Annia Hatch	9.481
Russia	Anna Pavlova	9.475
Russia	Elena Zamolodchikova	9.412
Democratic People's Republic of Korea (North Korea)	Yun-Mi Kang	9.381

MEN'S POMMEL HORSE

The pommel horse event uses a platform shaped like a horse's body. Attached to it are two handles called pommels. Gymnasts place only their hands on the horse. They swing their straightened legs in circular movements. Gymnasts end their routines with a handstand. They then land on the mat at the horse's side.

MAX WHITLOCK

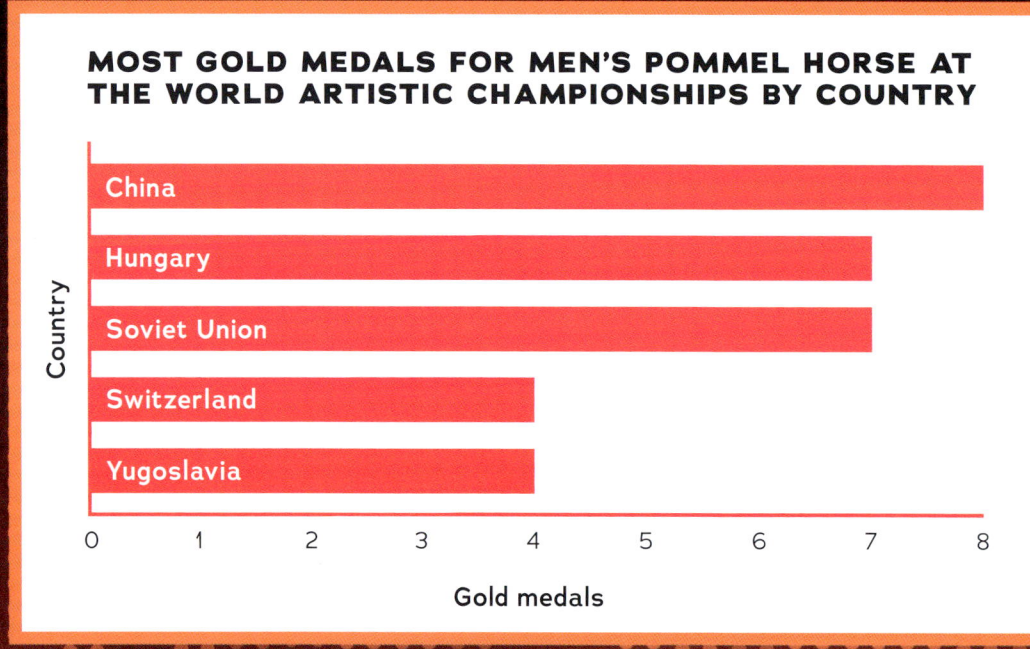

MOST GOLD MEDALS FOR MEN'S POMMEL HORSE AT THE WORLD ARTISTIC CHAMPIONSHIPS BY COUNTRY

WOMEN'S BALANCE BEAM

The balance beam is similar to the women's floor exercise. In both, gymnasts perform tumbling, acrobatics, and dance moves. But the balance beam has an extra challenge. The gymnast must make these moves on a beam of aluminum and foam padding 4.1 feet (1.2 m) off the ground. The beam is only 4 inches (10 cm) wide.

SHAWN JOHNSON

2008 OLYMPICS WOMEN'S BALANCE BEAM RESULTS

TEAM	GYMNAST	SCORE
United States	Shawn Johnson	16.225
United States	Nastia Liukin	16.025
China	Fei Cheng	15.950
Russia	Anna Pavlova	15.900
Romania	Gabriela Dragoi	15.625

MEN'S STILL RINGS

In men's still rings, two rings are suspended 9.2 feet (2.8 m) above a mat. Gripping the rings, the gymnast holds his arms and legs in many positions. He must move smoothly from one to the next. A dismount to the mat ends the routine. Upper body strength is important for this event.

YIBING CHEN

2008 OLYMPICS MEN'S STILL RINGS RESULTS

TEAM	GYMNAST	SCORE
China	Yibing Chen	16.600
China	Wei Yang	16.425
Ukraine	Oleksandr Vorobiov	16.325
Italy	Andrea Coppolino	16.225
France	Danny Pinheiro Rodrigues	16.225

Best All-Around

Winning an individual all-around competition is a badge of honor. All gymnasts start with a score of zero. They then perform one routine in each event. Adding their scores determines the women's and men's all-around winners. US gymnast Simone Biles is considered by many to be the G.O.A.T., or greatest of all time. She's won six World all-around gold medals!

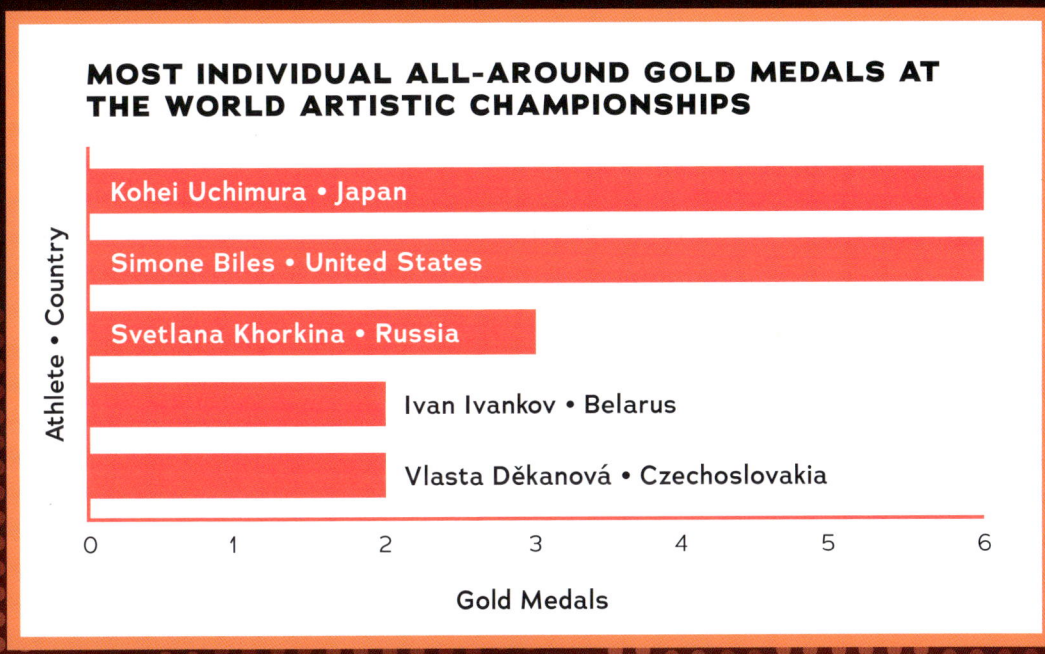

Wait, What!?

Simone Biles made the record books by winning 30 World Championships medals and seven Olympic medals. That's more than any other gymnast.

CHAPTER 2
TEAM STATS

SOVIET SUPERSTARS

The women's team from the Soviet Union had the longest Olympic winning streak in gymnastics history. Between 1952 and 1988, the Soviet team went to nine Olympic Games. Its members won 88 medals. These included nine golds in the team competition. In 1991, the Soviet Union's government collapsed. Its lands were broken up into 15 nations, including Russia.

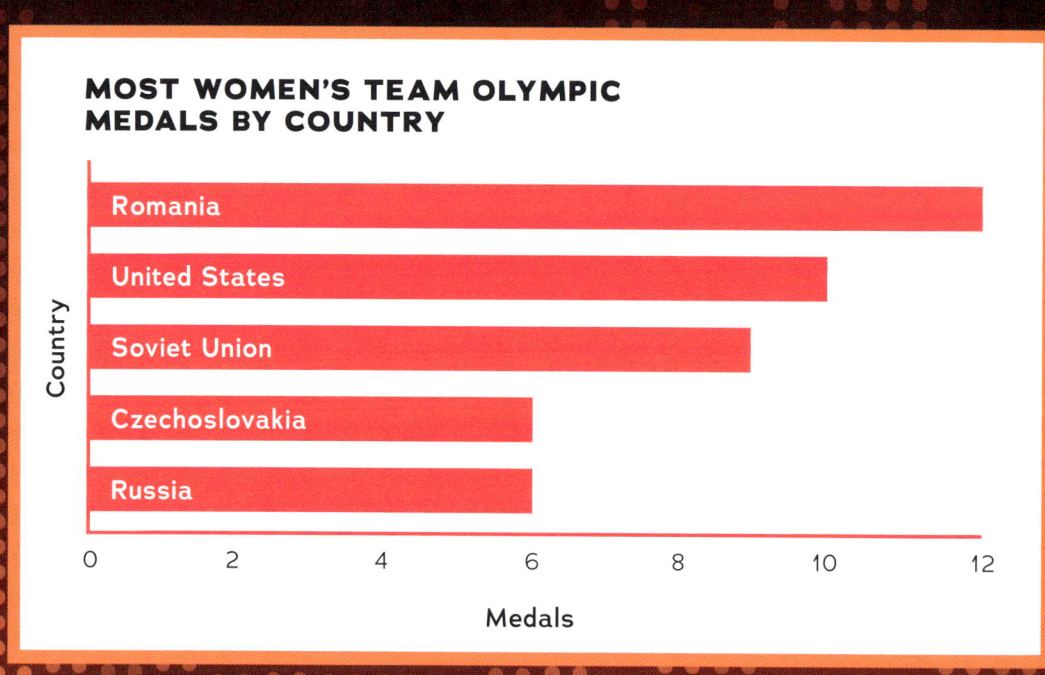

MOST WOMEN'S TEAM OLYMPIC MEDALS BY COUNTRY

Japan's Triumphs

Japan's men's gymnastics team was the best men's team from 1960 to 1976. It won five Olympic team gold medals in a row. In 2004, Japan returned to the top spot. They won the team gold again in 2016. They also scored the team silver in 2008, 2012, and 2020.

2016 OLYMPIC JAPANESE MEN'S TEAM

Wait, What!?

Shun Fujimoto helped Japan take team Olympic gold in 1976. He scored a career high of 9.7 on the still rings. He performed his routine with a broken kneecap.

CHINA ON THE RISE

The men's team from China has become one to watch. At the 2022 World Championships, China won the men's team competition with a score of 257.858. They beat Japan by 4.463 points. It was the largest margin between first and second place in 15 years.

CHINA AFTER WINNING THE MEN'S TEAM EVENT IN 2022

| MOST RECENT WORLD ARTISTIC CHAMPIONSHIPS MEN'S TEAM WINNERS ||
COUNTRY	YEAR
Japan	2023
China	2022
Russia	2019
China	2018
Japan	2015

USA GOLD

US women won their first team Olympic gold medal in 1996. The historic team was nicknamed the Magnificent Seven.

When the D score was introduced in 2006, it gave the US women's team a big advantage. US gymnasts are known for their strength and daring moves. They can get high scores by doing difficult routines. High D scores helped them win team gold medals at the 2012 and 2016 Olympics.

MAGNIFICENT SEVEN

MOST RECENT WORLD ARTISTIC CHAMPIONSHIPS WOMEN'S TEAM WINNERS	
COUNTRY	YEAR
United States	2023
United States	2022
United States	2019
United States	2018
United States	2015

Best Team Ever?

Many consider the 2016 US women's team the greatest of all time. Nicknamed the Final Five, they had the highest team score in all four events. They also won many medals outside their team victory. In the individual events, team members took home three golds, four silvers, and one bronze.

FINAL FIVE

ALEXANDRA RAISMAN

WOMEN'S TEAM USA INDIVIDUAL MEDAL WINNERS, 2016 OLYMPICS

EVENT	ATHLETE	D SCORE	E SCORE	TOTAL
GOLD				
Floor exercise	Simone Biles	6.900	9.066	15.966
Vault	Simone Biles	6.300	9.600	15.900
All-around	Simone Biles	25.700	36.498	62.198
SILVER				
Floor exercise	Alexandra Raisman	6.600	8.900	15.500
Balance beam	Lauren Hernandez	6.400	8.933	15.333
Uneven bars	Madison Kocian	6.700	9.133	15.833
All-around	Alexandra Raisman	25.100	34.998	60.098
BRONZE				
Balance beam	Simone Biles	6.500	8.233	14.733

CHAPTER 3
STATS ARE HERE TO STAY

RISKY MOVES

The modern scoring system affects how gymnasts train and build routines. To win, they need a high D score. It rewards difficult moves, so gymnasts often take risks. With these risks, though, they increase the chance for injury.

SHILESE JONES

2023 WORLD ARTISTIC CHAMPIONSHIPS WOMEN'S ALL-AROUND RANKINGS

RANK	GYMNAST	COUNTRY	SCORE
1	Simone Biles	United States	58.399
2	Rebeca Andrade	Brazil	56.766
3	Shilese Jones	United States	56.332
4	Qiyuan Qiu	China	54.799
5	Alice D'Amato	Italy	52.265

THE CODE OF POINTS

Athletes and coaches keep up to date on the Code of Points. This guide lists the difficulty points assigned to each move. The code changes about every four years. Gymnasts adjust their training with each change. This makes sure their routines can earn the most points possible.

ILLIA KOVTUN

2023 WORLD ARTISTIC CHAMPIONSHIPS MEN'S ALL-AROUND RANKINGS

RANK	GYMNAST	COUNTRY	SCORE
1	Daiki Hashimoto	Japan	86.132
2	Illia Kovtun	Ukraine	84.998
3	Frederick Richard	United States	84.332
4	Kenta Chiba	Japan	83.464
5	Milad Karimi	Kazakhstan	82.931

ALICE KINSELLA

QUESTIONING THE SCORING SYSTEM

Some gymnastics officials worry that the scoring system is too hard for fans to understand. They fear confused fans will lose interest in the sport. Some people want to get rid of the system. They want to return to the days of a single score and the perfect 10.

FOLLOWING THE STATS

Despite these fears, gymnastics fans aren't going anywhere. Most don't care that they don't know how every move is scored. Some gymnastics fans study the scoring system. Like other sports fans, they may pour over their favorite star's stats. But what many fans enjoy most is watching amazing gymnasts giving it their all.

A YOUNG FAN HOLDING UP A SIGN DURING AN OLYMPIC GYMNASTICS TRIAL

STATS MATCHUP

Daiki Hashimoto of Japan won the gold medal in the men's all-around at the 2020 Olympics. At the World Championships in 2021, many thought he would win. But Boheng Zhang of China beat Hashimoto by just .017 points. It was Zhang's first international competition.

BOHENG ZHANG

BOHENG ZHANG 2021 WORLD ARTISTIC CHAMPIONSHIPS RESULTS

EVENT	D SCORE	E SCORE	TOTAL
Floor exercise	6.300	8.583	14.883
Pommel horse	5.800	7.666	13.466
Still rings	6.100	8.500	14.600
Vault	5.600	9.266	14.866
Parallel bars	6.100	9.266	15.366
Horizontal bar	6.200	8.600	14.800
All-around	36.100	51.881	87.981

At the 2022 World Championships, Hashimoto reclaimed the all-around gold. Zhang got the silver. Hashimoto and Zhang are friendly rivals. They enjoy battling for the title of the world's leading male gymnast. So who's the best? Look at the stats and decide for yourself.

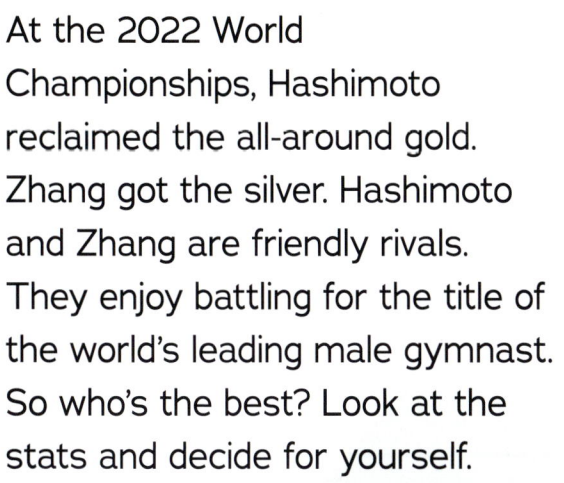

DAIKI HASHIMOTO

DAIKI HASHIMOTO 2022 WORLD ARTISTIC CHAMPIONSHIPS RESULTS

EVENT	D SCORE	E SCORE	TOTAL
Floor exercise	6.000	8.666	14.666
Pommel horse	6.000	8.333	14.333
Still rings	5.800	8.066	13.866
Vault	5.600	9.300	14.900
Parallel bars	6.100	8.900	15.000
Horizontal bar	6.000	8.433	14.433
All-around	35.500	51.698	87.198

Glossary

acrobatic: performed with leaps and other body movements

dismount: the movement a gymnast makes at the end of a routine

D score: the part of a gymnast's score that grades the difficulty of their routine

E score: the part of a gymnast's score that grades execution, or how well they perform each move

handstand: when a gymnast stands upright on their hands

mat: a soft pad for gymnastics

routine: the series of movements that a gymnast performs during a gymnastics event

springboard: a platform with springs

tumbling: movements such as rolls, twists, handsprings, or somersaults

Learn More

Anderson, Josh. *Simone Biles vs. Nadia Comaneci: Who Would Win?* Minneapolis: Lerner Publications, 2024.

Britannica Kids: Gymnastics
https://kids.britannica.com/kids/article/gymnastics/353221

Kiddle: Gymnastics Facts for Kids
https://kids.kiddle.co/Gymnastics

Lawrence, Blythe. *Trailblazing Women in Gymnastics*. Chicago: Norwood House, 2023.

Levit, Joe. *Gymnastics's G.O.A.T: Nadia Comaneci, Simone Biles, and More*. Minneapolis: Lerner Publications, 2022.

Monnig, Alex. *Gymnastics*. Minneapolis: A & D Extreme, 2023.

INDEX

all-around, 17, 23–25

Biles, Simone, 17, 23–24

Code of Points, 25

dance moves, 7, 15

D score, 5, 21, 23–24

E score, 5, 23

Final Five, 22

judges, 4–5

Magnificent Seven, 21

perfect 10, 11, 26

release, 8–9

routine, 5–8, 13–14, 16–17, 19, 21, 24–25

tumbling, 7, 15

PHOTO ACKNOWLEDGMENTS

Image credits: Tim Clayton/Corbis via Getty Images, pp. 4, 6, 12, 24; Jeff Pachoud/AFP via Getty Images, p. 5; Eileen Langsley/Popperfoto via Getty Images, pp. 7, 29; Wang Lili/Xinhua via Getty Images, p. 8; Kyodo News via Getty Images, p. 9; Ian MacNicol/Getty Images, p. 10; Vladimir Rys/Bongarts/Getty Images, p. 13; Ben Stansall/AFP via Getty Images, p. 14; Bob Rosato /Sports Illustrated via Getty Images, p. 15; Clive Brunskill/Getty Images, p. 16; Thomas Coex/AFP via Getty Images, p. 19; Paul Ellis/AFP via Getty Images, p. 20; Doug Pensinger/Allsport, p. 21; Alex Livesey/Getty Images, pp. 22–23; Zheng Huansong/Xinhua via Getty Images, p. 25; Laurence Griffiths/Getty Images, p. 26; Carmen Mandato/Getty Images, p. 27; Du Xiaoyi/Xinhua via Getty Images, p. 28. Design Elements: Ali Kahfi/Getty Images; Sarayut Thaneerat/Getty Images.

Cover: Melissa J. Perenson/Cal Sport Media/AP Photo.